Audio Access Included

PLAYBACK+
Speed • Pitch • Balance • Loop

CELLO

Classic Pop Songs

Audio arrangements by Peter Deneff

To access audio visit:
www.halleonard.com/mylibrary
Enter Code
6780-2205-7480-3087

ISBN 978-1-5400-0252-5

7777 W. BLUEMOUND RD. P.O. BOX 13819 MILWAUKEE, WI 53213

Visit Hal Leonard Online at
www.halleonard.com

BRIDGE OVER TROUBLED WATER

CELLO

Words and Music by
PAUL SIMON

CANDLE IN THE WIND

CELLO

Words and Music by ELTON JOHN
and BERNIE TAUPIN

DUST IN THE WIND

CELLO

Words and Music by
KERRY LIVGREN

EVERY BREATH YOU TAKE

CELLO

Music and Lyrics by
STING

FIRE AND RAIN

CELLO

Words and Music by
JAMES TAYLOR

HAVE I TOLD YOU LATELY

CELLO

Words and Music by
VAN MORRISON

GOOD VIBRATIONS

CELLO

Words and Music by BRIAN WILSON
and MIKE LOVE

HEAVEN

CELLO

Words and Music by BRYAN ADAMS
and JIM VALLANCE

13

LEAN ON ME

CELLO

Words and Music by
BILL WITHERS

SHE'S ALWAYS A WOMAN

CELLO

Words and Music by
BILLY JOEL

WITH A LITTLE HELP FROM MY FRIENDS

CELLO

Words and Music by JOHN LENNON
and PAUL McCARTNEY

TEARS IN HEAVEN

CELLO

Words and Music by ERIC CLAPTON
and WILL JENNINGS